My Best Moment

Four Personal Narratives

by Olivia Vega, Michael Martinoff,
Nadel Henville, and Kunal Rai

Table of Contents

Personal Narratives

What is a personal narrative?

A personal narrative is a nonfiction text that recreates an experience from the author's life. A personal narrative has a strong point of view, usually in the first person. It also communicates a distinct mood, or overall feeling. Most personal narratives are about something "big" in the author's life, such as a proud or sad moment, a trip or adventure, or an event that changed attitudes or actions.

What is the purpose of a personal narrative?

A personal narrative is a way to describe an experience so that others feel like they were there. Writers do this by using sensory details—what they saw, heard, touched, smelled, and tasted—and by including important events, characters, and dialogue. Writers explain what happened and also tell what they were thinking at the time and how they felt.

How do you read a personal narrative?

The title will likely give you a clue about the experience that the author will describe. As you read, pay close attention to the sequence of events. Ask yourself: *Did this event happen to the person, or did the person make it happen? How did this event affect the person's life? Is the author simply writing to entertain, or is there something that I can learn from his or her experience?*

A personal narrative focuses on one particular incident in the author's life.

A personal narrative may be a few paragraphs or several pages in length.

A personal narrative includes specific details about the time, place, and people involved.

Features of a Personal Narrative

A personal narrative includes the author's thoughts and feelings as well as the actual events.

A personal narrative includes dialogue.

Who writes personal narratives?

Everyone does! People record their experiences in diaries and journals, and share them in letters and e-mails. These informal writing opportunities provide valuable practice in selecting just the right details to make the experience come alive for others.

Meet the Authors

"My Brown-Eyed Babe"

Name: Olivia Vega

School: Wellington Christian Academy

Wellington, Kansas

About Me: I like to hang out with friends and I like to run. I want to be an artist or an author.

"The Hammock"

Name: Michael Martinoff

School: Grandhaven Elementary

McMinnville, Oregon

About Me: I like to play baseball and travel. My mom thinks I'm funny.

"Nazaih Arrives"

Name: Nadel Henville

School: Mayberry Elementary

East Hartford, Connecticut

About Me: I was born on the island of St. Lucia. I want to live in Paris when I grow up.

Tools Writers Use
A Strong Lead

A strong lead, or first sentence, grabs, or "hooks" the reader. A strong lead makes the reader want to keep reading. The lead describes something important about the topic without telling too much about the good parts to come. For personal narratives, writers usually use an indirect lead. An indirect lead may quote someone, ask a question, or describe a setting.

"The Catch"

Name: Kunal Rai

School: Old Union Elementary

Southlake, Texas

About Me: I would like to become an inventor and discover a way for all things to be powered by clean energy.

My Brown-Eyed Babe

Did Juliet know she was so cute? I patted her furry yellow head. Then I went to my friend Lakin's house. We were having a sleepover.

Juliet is my dog. She is an English setter. She is blond. She is covered with orange spots. My Juliet has the **floppiest** ears ever! I wish she didn't have a sad look all the time. Now was a time to be happy.

Juliet had her own home in the garage. She had her own pillow. She had a blanket. Her dog house did not look comfortable to me. But I am not a dog. For her it was a palace.

I came home from the sleepover. My little brother, Isaiah, ran to me. He yelled, "Juliet had puppies! Six of them!" My heart was racing. I ran to the garage.

I stopped right in front of the puppies. I looked them over. What a happy moment! One black puppy caught my eye. She was alone in a corner. Her eyes were shut. Aw, she was so sweet. She had the **tiniest** brown eyebrows. I picked her up. Once this puppy was in my arms, I knew she was going to be my dog. I talked softly into her ear. "I will never let you go. You will be my brown-eyed babe."

The days went by. Weeks and months passed. For all that time, my brown-eyed babe stayed with me. She sat on my lap. She sat by my side. After three months, I came up with her name. It was kind of silly. But I thought the name fit her. I picked up the puppy. I held her close to my face. "Maya Moo Mercedes," I said. She liked the name! After I said it, she licked my nose.

Maya had one sister and four brothers. Jewels was the girl. Max, Marshmallow, Julian, and Milkshake were the boys.

One day my mom put her arm on my shoulder. "We're going to have a garage sale . . . and we're going to give away the puppies."

"What? No, not Maya!" I shouted. I felt my heart break. "Can't we keep her?" I asked hopefully.

"Isaiah already asked to keep Max," Mom said.

No! This could not be. Not after all the times I slept with Maya on the kitchen floor. All the time I spent making up silly songs for her. Was it all for nothing? "That's not fair!" I said, trying to change Mom's mind.

"I can't tell Isaiah 'no,' now," Mom explained. "I already told him 'yes.'"

"We can keep both!" I said. "That way no one will feel bad! Come on, Mom! Please?" I said.

Mom sighed. She saw that I loved Maya. "Okay," she finally said. She smiled.

Garage-sale day came. We set out the other puppies. I held my breath as the first people came. One person picked up Julian. He said, "I'll take this one." I was sad that Julian was now gone. After a few hours, the other puppies were gone. Juliet had the right to feel sad now, I thought.

I picked up Maya from my lap. I told her softly, "I will *never* let you go. You are my brown-eyed babe." I brushed her fur. I kissed her head. I put her on her pillow. Then I closed the door behind me.

* * * * *

It's been a year since Maya was born. She has been by my side ever since. A few weeks ago, Maya had three puppies. They are beautiful. They are the **most precious** things I have ever seen. I fell in love with them, too. But it doesn't matter how many puppies Maya has. It doesn't matter how old she will get. Maya will always be my brown-eyed babe.

Max on floor; Maya lying on Juliet

The Hammock

Do you have a special place? A place where you go to get away from everything? A place to relax? I do. It's the hammock in my backyard.

My favorite time of year there is fall. I lie back in the hammock. I look at the trees swaying. I see the **bluest** of skies. I watch the leaves fall. I love it when the red, yellow, and orange leaves float onto my face.

Sometimes I bring out my mp3 player. I listen to music while I watch the leaves. Other times, I just listen to the creak of the hammock. It moves back and forth, back and forth. Ahh . . .

Sometimes I bring a book. Stories set in a forest are the most fun. Being in the hammock among the trees makes me feel like I'm in the story. If I'm reading an action scene, I imagine that I'm with the good guys. I pretend they are jumping around. They say to me, "The bad guys are weak. You can take them!"

I love the smell of the trees, too. I never realized before that trees could smell so good. When I'm in my hammock, I often close my eyes. I sniff the air. I catch the smell of pine trees. I breathe in deeply. Ahh . . .

Once in a while, my dog hops up onto the hammock with me. Fritz is a beagle-labrador mix. The hammock wobbles for a couple of seconds. I steady it. Fritz licks me. I pet him with the softest, **gentlest** strokes.

Your **most special** place doesn't have to be a hammock. But I do hope you find a place where you can drift away to another world.

Reread the Personal Narratives

Analyze the Narratives
- What experiences do these personal narratives describe?
- Where did they happen? How did each setting affect what happened?
- Which people were involved? How did these people affect what happened?
- How do the writers feel about their experiences now?

Analyze the Tools Writers Use: A Strong Lead
- What type of lead did Olivia use? Michael?
- Did the leads "hook" you as a reader? Why? How?
- What did you think the narratives were going to be about from the lead?

Focus on Words: Superlatives
Superlatives are special adjectives that are used to compare three or more things. Some superlatives end in **-est**, while others are preceded by the word **most**. Analyze the following superlatives from "My Brown-Eyed Babe" and "The Hammock."

Adjective	Superlative Form of the Adjective	Page
floppy	floppiest	6
tiny	tiniest	7
precious	most precious	9
blue	bluest	10
gentle	gentlest	12
special	most special	12

13

Nazaih Arrives

The **greatest** day of my life was December 18, 2008. It was a cold, gray day. Outside it was raining. Inside I was a burst of sunshine. That day my nephew Nazaih was born! This was not my first time as an aunt. But it was the first time I went to the hospital to see the newborn baby.

Everyone in my family was excited. We wanted to see my sister Natalia and her baby. At first, we couldn't find the right room. That was our **most anxious** moment. Then we found the room. Baby presents were all over the floor. Natalia was in bed. Nazaih was next to her. He looked so tiny. But he weighed eight pounds and eleven ounces. That's pretty big for a newborn.

Everyone held Nazaih but me. I felt a little left out. Then I got over it. I was happy to look at the baby. In fact, I couldn't take my eyes off him. Nazaih had hazel eyes. He had soft, smooth skin. He had lots of hair. My family called him "Little Man." That's because he had the **hairiest** arms and legs. He was the cutest when he yawned. I couldn't stop staring. My heart melted.

Natalia was in pain. We let her be. I did not get to see Nazaih again until later in the day. As I looked at my baby nephew, I thought about his future. What would he be like as a toddler? I saw him playing with a basketball set, laughing. I thought about the games I would play with him. I hoped he would like hide and seek.

When I went home, I felt a new kind of happiness. It was like a dark hole in me was now filled up with Nazaih.

The Catch

A cold wind blew through the ballpark that Saturday night in October 2007. My baseball team, the Raptors, was playing the Mountain Cats. It was the playoffs. The Mountain Cats were the **toughest** team in the league. It was do-or-die for us.

The weather was cool. But the bats were hot. In the sixth inning the score was 13–12. We were on top! The Mountain Cats' came up. It was their last licks.

We took the field. We were not going to let the other team shake our spirit. We got two outs. Then the Cats loaded the bases! What's worse, their **fiercest** hitter was up. Jack walked onto the field swinging his bat. The crowd cheered as he walked toward the plate. Our stony determination began to show some cracks.

Jack took his place in the batter's box. He got set. The lights flickered. The crowd went quiet. Tyler, our pitcher, wound up. He threw a fastball right down the middle. "Strike one," yelled the umpire.

The author focuses on one specific event. The actual incident that inspired this personal narrative, a baseball game, was only a couple of hours in the author's life.

I was in center field. I took many steps back. I could tell that Jack was going for a homer.

Tyler threw a ball down the middle again. *Crack!* The baseball zoomed past Tyler. It kept on going. The lights flickered again. The crowd roared again. The ball was coming my way! I was the most nervous person on the field. I ran in a few steps. Then I ran backward. I wasn't sure where the ball would land. The crowd grew quiet again.

Here the author shares his thoughts and feelings while he was on the field, as well as the actual events that occurred.

The Catch

I jumped into the air. *Thump!* Something hit my glove. I fell to the ground. *Thud!* I skidded. I rolled. My jersey was covered with dirt and grass. I was afraid to look in my glove. Then I saw my teammates jump for joy. They ran toward me. I looked into the glove. There was the ball!

Using sound words helps readers feel as if they're right there with the author.

"Out!" yelled the umpire. I jumped into the air. I did a 1440 spin (that's four 360 degree spins). My teammates ran to me. They gave me a group hug. The umpire said the game was over. We had won. Both teams came out of the dugouts. We shook hands.

The author brings in other people that were at the event, and uses dialogue and detailed descriptions to help place the readers in the middle of the action.

Our team gathered around the coach. We reviewed the game, which we always do. But now we bubbled over with excitement. We were in the finals! It had been a long, hard road. The coach handed me the game ball. I was voted MVP. I still wasn't sure if it had been a dream.

A personal narrative is about an experience that has a deep, personal meaning for the author. In the end, the author shares how he felt after the experience and his hopes for the future.

The stands cleared out. People were leaving the park. I looked around. I thought about my catch. Helping my team win was one of the **most phenomenal** experiences of my life. On the way home, I wondered if I would be able to make a catch like that again. All I could do was keep practicing and hope for another chance.

Kunal keeps the ball he caught as a memory of his best moment.

Reread the Personal Narratives

Analyze the Narratives
- What experiences do these personal narratives describe?
- Where did they happen? How did each setting affect what happened?
- Which people were involved? How did these people affect what happened?
- How do the writers feel about their experiences now?

Analyze the Tools Writers Use: A Strong Lead
- What type of lead did Nadel use? Kunal?
- Did the leads "hook" you as a reader? Why? How?
- What did you think the narrative was going to be about from the lead?

Focus on Words: Superlatives
Superlatives are special adjectives that are used to compare three or more things. Some superlatives end in **-est**, while others are preceded by the word **most**. Analyze the following superlatives from "Nazaih Arrives" and "The Catch."

Adjective	Superlative Form of the Adjective	Page
great	greatest	14
anxious	most anxious	14
hairy	hairiest	15
tough	toughest	16
fierce	fiercest	17
phenomenal	most phenomenal	20

How does an author write a

Personal Narrative?

Reread "The Catch" and think about what Kunal Rai did to write this narrative. How did he keep a narrow focus? How did he make you feel like you were there?

1. Decide on an Experience

Remember: A personal narrative is an actual retelling of something you have experienced. Therefore, you will use words such as **I**, **me**, and **my** as you write. In "The Catch," the author wanted to tell about an amazing play he made for his baseball team.

2. Decide Who Else Needs to Be in Your Narrative

Often, other people—or even animals—were a part of your experience. Ask yourself:
• Who was there with me?
• Which people are important to my story?
• How will I describe these people?
• Which people should I leave out?
• Can I tell my story without embarrassing another person?
  If not, what other experience could I write about?

Person	Jack	Tyler	Umpire	Teammates and Coach
Importance to Story	fiercest hitter on the opposing team	pitcher on the author's team	called the batter out and let the players know the game was over	congratulated the author; gave him the MVP award

3. Recall Events and Setting

Jot down notes about what happened and where it happened. Ask yourself:
- Where did my experience take place? How will I describe it?
- What was the situation or problem I experienced? Was the experience happy, scary, sad, or surprising?
- What events happened?
- How did my experience turn out?
- What questions might my readers have about my experience that I could answer in my narrative?

Setting	Events	How My Experience Turned Out
Baseball field at Bicentennial Park **Situation or Problem** My team wanted to beat the Mountain Cats in the league semifinals.	1. The Cats' fiercest hitter was up when they were down by one run and had the bases loaded. 2. The hitter hit the ball straight out to center field where I stood. 3. I jumped into the air to catch the ball.	I caught it! We won the game, I got the MVP award, and our team got to go to the finals.

Glossary

bluest   (BLOO-est) having the most color blue (page 10)

fiercest   (FEER-sist) most terrifying (page 17)

floppiest   (FLAH-pee-est) softest; loosest (page 6)

gentlest   (JEN-tuh-lest) most delicate (page 12)

greatest   (GRAY-test) best (page 14)

hairiest   (HAIR-ee-est) having the most hair (page 15)

most anxious   (MOST ANK-shus) most worrisome (page 14)

most phenomenal   (MOST fih-NAH-muh-nul) most amazing (page 20)

most precious   (MOST PREH-shus) most cherished (page 9)

most special   (MOST SPEH-shul) most valued (page 12)

tiniest   (TY-nee-est) smallest (page 7)

toughest   (TUH-fest) most challenging (page 16)